With [illegible] prayer the
Lord will
strengthen you
to finish what
His called you
to do.
[signature]

Adopted
↑
Mother & daughter
From Jersey

Met @
Conference
"2018"

What People Are Saying About *The Power To Keep Going*

Sharon Beth Brani, has absolutely knocked the ball clear out of the park with her new book "The Power to Keep Going". Inside the covers of this brilliant book, we are left spellbound by her heartwarming and encouraging stories of triumph. Not only do we learn how to deal with difficult circumstances but are empowered to reign over them. I would recommend this book to anyone who wants to add more life to their years.

Thomas G. Sowell, Owner/Author of the Blog "The Wise Man of Navidad".
Texas

If you need a stronger belief system and heartfelt compassion to develop your life then connect to the emotional intelligence that Sharon Brani brings in her writing and coaching.

Brent O'Bannon, World's First Gallup Certified Strengths Coach, Championing Strengths for Global Excellence.
Texas

An encouraging, informative work for those in need of strategies when trials and emptiness plague the soul. Board Certified Life Coach, Sharon Brani addresses core issues of the heart with proven strategies to help you live your best life now.

Valerie Caraotta, Freelance Writer.
Georgia

Sharon Beth Brani engages in holy listening and sharing of her wisdom every day to those who are fortunate to have her as a personal coach and guide. Through the pages of this book, Sharon's personal and powerful message can now influence and encourage you and me, too. Her message is one of perseverance, hope, and - most of all - faith.

Bradley Davidson, Personal Coach and Spiritual Director.
Oklahoma

We lived so many of the experiences Sharon relates in her wonderful story of God's redemption for defeated and discouraged people. Her genuine understanding and compassion expresses God's faithfulness with a focused plan following His precepts. As a couple, we were at the end of our marriage. With Sharon's gentle but firm help, we are enjoying the very best years of our lives together. God IS Great!

Richard and Carolyn Smith,
Virginia

This book is truly inspiring and unbelievably encouraging! It embodies the reality that life can be hard but it gives advice on how to keep going when times get tough.

Noelle Brani, Photographer
Virginia

As a family doctor for 20 years, I was very attuned to promoting wellness in people, but usually consumed by controlling chronic illness in so many of them. As a palliative/hospice physician in the past 10 years, I have had the privilege to daily experience through the journey of those at the end of life, what is important in life. Sharon Brani's honest and transparent work shines a light of hope on both. I have been intrigued by the concept of hope as a physician for years, even more as I care for people at the end of life. Sharon elegantly, through story, helps us to understand that hope, like love and faith, is a gift. It is freely given, generously given, and ours to receive, just in the accepting, by opening our hearts. So many patients have taught me that in the end, it's not about what you're hoping for, but who you're hoping in. Sharon has lived that, claimed that, and shares that profoundly and pointedly in this honest journey from the head to the heart.

Timothy B. Short, MD, FAAFP, FAAHPM Associate
Professor, Palliative Care.
Virginia

In her new book, The Power to Keep Going, author, Sharon Brani, speaks of God's amazing grace. Sharon, herself, experienced amazing grace as she wrote this powerful book. She does a masterful job of illustrating how, when we feel at our lowest, God meets us there and gives us the strength to look up, reach out, and rise above the depths we sometimes find ourselves in. I am impressed with the sensitivity and encouragement this book offers and pray that many will be uplifted and helped by reading it.

Sally Chambers, Author of "The Stonekeepers".

Florida

The Power
To Keep Going

Also By Sharon Beth Brani

Always Remember

The Unforgettable Christmas Journey

The Power

To Keep Going

Sharon Beth Brani

 ISBN:

978-0-692-06647-8

Cover by Noelle Brani Photography

This book is dedicated to all those longing for strength and renewal.

Preface

It wasn't the first time I had run a long distance race, but it was the longest race. Ten miles. From the moment the race began, my heart pounded with excitement. I had trained well. I knew the winding route through one of my favorite cities, Charlottesville, Virginia. My body was in good shape. I was prepared.

But even though I knew all these things, I wondered, "Would I be able to keep going?"

After a fast start, I settled in at a comfortable speed and paced myself. Step by step. Mile by mile. From time to time I slowed my steps and gulped down some water. Refreshment. But the refreshment was short lived. Even though I paced myself, I began to feel weary. My reserves felt depleted. Suddenly I began to wonder if I had it in me to complete the race.

Doubts loomed like monsters in my mind. Should I slow to a walk? Deep down inside this crazy thought screamed for attention: "You can't do it. You can't!" Over and over and over.

Suddenly I heard the sound of a band playing a

familiar march. Sweat running down my face, my eyes searched, looking for where the music was coming from. Drumbeats. Energy. Trumpets cheering the runners on. My steps picked up as I got in rhythm with the music. No longer was I overcome with doubts. Instead, renewed energy and resolve overtook me. Then suddenly up ahead I saw it - the finish line. And I knew that I could make it the whole way.

Life has some long and difficult stretches. Even though we do our best to pace ourselves, we suddenly find ourselves doubting we can complete what we set out to do. Goals are ignored. Plans are neglected. That cherished dream is discarded along the path and forgotten.

Yes, we want to quit. We want to give up. Discouragement sets in.

But the truth is, there is power to keep going through all the ups and downs of life. Even though we may have to adjust the season and how we accomplish the dream, we can keep on. Because God promises to not only give us the strength to keep going, but He becomes our strength.

Let me share with you about this amazing power to keep going. No longer need you become defeated and discouraged. No longer do you need to stop running the race and lay aside your dreams. Instead, you'll find yourself dreaming more and running more because you've discovered God's power, and He is yours - and life becomes an adventure.

Table of Contents

Introduction

I love the words of Eric Liddell, renowned Scotsman Olympic winner, who when asked "Where does the power to keep going come from?" clearly and confidently answered, "From within." He took seriously the words of Scripture that "if you seek the Lord with all your heart, you will find Him" (Jeremiah 29:13). To believe, he asserted, was to believe with the mind and the heart, to accept and to act accordingly on that basis. Liddell credited his fast race to the Lord of his life. For those of us living many years later, the key of putting our trust in the Lord is the same.

There have been times in my life when I have questioned if I had enough strength to go on. Sometimes I felt completely depleted and empty. There was no power. There was no strength. There was no human will to overcome. But in my place of great need, I have discovered God's greatness and His strength. Looking back, it's clear that it was my helplessness and hopelessness that drew me to the One who whispers again and again, "I am your Shepherd. I am all that you need."

Although there are many things that I do not

understand, I know that His Word is true and that He is always faithful. His power can be seen shining like a steady beacon to our hurting and confused world. It speaks truth, and also points the way for us to keep going today, no matter how difficult our personal situations might be.

Is your life difficult right now? Are you struggling to know how to handle it? Join me now over the next few pages as we glance at the stories of those who have discovered an amazing truth. Like Liddell, they experienced God's power when they desperately needed Him.

What they discovered can also be yours. Their stories remind you that God is faithful. He also reaches out in love to you, no matter how deep your pit, and will empower you with all that you need as you seek Him.

Chapter 1

When Life Leaves You Empty

You are my hiding place; You will protect me from trouble and surround me with songs of deliverance.
~Psalm 32:7 (NIV)

When I was in my teens I first read the story of Corrie ten Boom, a Dutch watchmaker and Christian whose family helped many Jews escape the Nazi holocaust during World War II. She spent time in prison for her actions and was miraculously released due to a "clerical error." Corrie was often referred to as a Tramp for the Lord, because she spent her life going place to place telling people about Him. She spent the remaining years of her life sharing the love of Jesus and the hope that is found in Him with numerous people. She not only wrote many books, but in 1971 her bestselling book "The Hiding Place" was made into a movie and released by World Wide Pictures in 1975.

I'll never forget that night when I saw "The Hiding

Place", starring Jeannette Clift in the role of Corrie. It was the first movie that I had ever seen, and as I entered the packed auditorium that night my heart beat loud with excitement. I had read many of Corrie ten Boom's books and knew that I was in for a moving experience. But I had no idea. From the beginning I was drawn into this story of love and forgiveness. And I walked out that night inspired as I realized that God worked in our lives through the darkest of circumstances. I was, and continue to be, in awe of His amazing grace, particularly when life leaves you empty.

There are times in all of our lives when we might experience emptiness. And although our stories might not be as dramatic as Corrie's, the realization of His forever care and provision is the same. Whether we're sitting alone in an airport terminal or a hospital waiting room, He is there. His love keeps reaching whether we are aware of it or not.

Years ago when I was a child we moved. Alot. My dad worked for IBM, and every few years we left the familiar for the unfamiliar. New schools. New homes. New churches. It was difficult for me to adjust and always took time. Letting go of the old and embracing the new. I'd oftentimes feel empty and alone and, I didn't know what to do with the emptiness. But early in my life, I had been taught about the One who would never leave you or forsake you (Joshua1:9).

My heart clung to that truth, so on the school bus sometimes I'd move over in my seat, making room for my best Friend. It seemed that just doing that made me feel a little better and somehow eased the ache, making it possible for me to handle one more day in the new school.

Corrie ten Boom shared about a power that enabled her to keep going. She spoke of prayer as being a place where you leave your helplessness and enter a realm where "with God all things are possible." Nothing is too great for Him. No problem is too big.

Today I often hear from people who are overwhelmed with life's difficulties. Discouragement and depression abound. But it's that same awareness of His power to cover us in the hardest of situations that changes everything. Knowing the One with Whom all things are possible changes us and gives us strength when our human strength is depleted. Transforming our thinking from irrational to rational is healing, and gives us hope that endures the toughest of challenges.

Yes, Corrie ten Boom experienced His power and so can we. So even if we're feeling defeated, depressed, and discouraged, there is a way to change. No one is without hope. There is power available to keep going. Others have discovered it, and so can you.

Chapter 2

Defeated, Depressed, and Discouraged

May the God of hope fill you with all joy and peace as you trust in Him, so that you may overflow with hope by the power of the Holy Spirit. ~Romans 15:13 (NIV)

I was in my eighth grade geometry class struggling to understand what seemed like Greek to me. I worked hard. Night after night I sweated through hours and hours of homework. So when my class took our first big test of the year, I thought surely I had passed. But I was wrong. As a matter of fact, that test had more red on it than anything else. Gulp. I glanced up to the right hand corner and saw my flunking grade. Quickly I hid my test. Embarrassment flooded over me, and for a few moments I just wanted a hole to open up and make me disappear.

"How in the world could I ever go on?" I thought. Up until then schoolwork had always come easily. Now I was defeated, discouraged, and most certainly depressed.

Looking back, I realize that it was only a momentary setback. That failing grade did not define me, but at that point in my life I didn't realize that. No, I was hopelessly trapped into seeing myself as a failing grade, and I felt defeated and discouraged.

Today many folks define themselves by their looks, their income, their job, or some other characteristic. None of those things define you though. You've been created in the image of God, and He says that you have value to Him. He sent His One and only Son to die for you and me while we were sinners.

We might lose our beauty. Life, and particularly aging, leaves a mark on all of us. But God still loves you. Finances might disappear. Your job might change. Your health might fail. All of these are changes in your circumstances, not you. You are loved with an everlasting love, and through it all, God continues to be with you and for you, whether you realize it or not.

When I was in high school, I heard the tragic story of Joni Eareckson Tada. When she was seventeen, a diving accident left her a quadriplegic in a wheelchair. During rehabilitation, she learned to type and paint with a brush between her teeth. Her first book, "Joni," the story of her life, was published in 1976 and sold more than four million copies. Eventually it was translated into more than 50 languages. Through her ministry, Joni and Friends, she began sharing the love of Jesus with millions of people with disabilities. In 1982, she married Ken Tada and today continues to influence the world with her thoughts about suffering, death, and divine healing. Her life is a shining example of one who has learned to truly live with joy when she could have stayed defeated, discouraged, and depressed.

How did she move from devastation, despair, and defeat to making such a great impact in life, particularly in the lives of those with disabilities? Joni admittedly struggled for a few years with anger and depression, but she began to change her focus. She noticed the impact of scores of friends from her church who rallied around her giving practical assistance. She saw that although her anger and depression made sense, she was still alive. And her life mattered.

With fresh resolve and a lot of hard work, Joni began to do what she could with what she had and discovered that even without fingers to type, she could write a book. And with a brush held between her teeth, she could create beautiful paintings. In that process of doing what she could, Joni began to live a new life, and many doors opened to her.

As a result, she continues to bless and influence so many people today all around the world.

You may not be facing life in a wheelchair, yet life's unpredictable storms may have you at a place where you're defeated, discouraged and depressed. Maybe it's been a long time since you've sensed God's presence, and things keep getting worse. Hold on, my friend. Remember, joy comes in the morning. Always.

Although today may be dark and you see nothing to encourage you, He has promised to never leave you or forsake you (Joshua 1:9). He loves you with an everlasting love (Jeremiah 31:3). And He will strengthen you and help you as you seek Him with all your heart. For that is when you will find Him (Jeremiah 29:13).

Yes, there is always a place to consult with a doctor if you are struggling with depression. It's important to reach out to others and let them know. Most of all turn to the Lord and seek His help, which enables you to tap into His power and strength.

Getting physical exercise has an immediate impact.

Begin walking outside or go to a gym. Set goals for the week. Practice kindness. These activities lead to clearer thinking and a more positive spirit. Above all, get physical rest. More often than not, those who feel defeated and discouraged are exhausted from not getting a good night's rest. Getting enough sleep makes such a difference.

There are other things to do for self care. Eat nutritious meals. Intentionally laugh and watch comedy. Just beginning to change your life's patterns can go a long way to reduce a sense of discouragement. Talk to a pastor, counselor, or friend and realize that you are not alone. Feelings of depression can be isolating and cause one to think that no one would understand. But the opposite is the truth. Feelings of despair, depression, and discouragement are common human reactions, and can be temporary with the proper help.

Feelings aren't permanent, so it's important to keep going in spite of discouraging feelings. If faced with trauma and crisis in one's life, like Joni faced, a huge adjustment must be made. A healthy resilience involves working to change one's perspective to build on one's strengths and see possibilities in addition to loss.

My experience of getting an unexpected low grade, although devastating to me at the time, was temporary. As soon as the teacher explained that since the whole class had done poorly on that geometry test, he was giving a retake, my spirits rose and I saw what I needed to do. I could influence the outcome. So I studied and worked hard to understand my mistakes and do better the next time. I can also remember my relief when I saw my grade - the result of all my hard work.

Joni's experience of keeping going in the midst of such devastation is an example to all of us. While she could have chosen to give up and live a life filled with bitterness and regret, she chose to allow the Lord to be her strength. As a result, her life is a shining testimony of triumph over tragedy.

Chapter 3

Discovering Power That Never Disappoints

But thanks be to God, who always leads us as captives in Christ's triumphal procession and uses us to spread the aroma of the knowledge of Him everywhere. ~2 Corinthians 2:14 (NIV)

If you've ever faced great disappointment in your life, you know how devastating it can be. I've experienced my share of disappointments that, at the time, seemed great. Not getting chosen for a much-longed-for part in a play. The loss of a special friendship. The rejection of a book manuscript. Again and again. But looking back, I realize those were rather small setbacks. But one heavy blow that was more difficult for me to overcome happened when I was young with a heart filled with hopes and dreams.

From the time I was a very young girl, I loved playing with dolls. Hour after hour I spent dressing them, talking with them and all the while I was dreaming of that time in my life when I would hold and rock my own sweet-smelling little one. Nothing seemed to give me as much joy as imagining myself as a mother. I often spent hours dreaming about that small Cape Cod house surrounded by a white picket fence. And in my youthful imagination, I could see the happy faces of lots of children smiling as they looked out the windows. Six children, at least. But then there was the day I sat in a doctor's office and heard those words: No chance of having a child of my own. Words that burned deep within my tender heart filled with dreams of being a mommy. Words that ripped my dearest hopes to shreds. Looking back, I remember my crushed spirit. Even though I went to another doctor who quickly assured me that it was not so, and that I would be able to have a child, that disappointment never went away. No, I always wondered if what I wanted more than anything would ever happen. And if not, how could I possibly go on? Was there a power to keep moving forward? Or would I become one of the walking dead - alive in body, but dead in spirit? It certainly could have happened to me, sensitive as I was. The Spirit tenderly comforted me day by day, breathing hope within me - a hope that somehow I was not forgotten by God. It was years until this hope was tested and tried, as if by fire.

Disappointment rips the spirit, and only when we

move forward does the deep pain begin to mend. V. Raymond Edman wisely shares that there is a disappointment that would destroy us unless we allow it to lift us upward toward a life of devotion to the Lord. Why go on, we wonder? Why?

I'm reminded how even the Apostle Paul experienced disappointment when he waited and waited for Titus to come (II Corinthians 2:12-14) at the old city of Troas, but he never came. Although we're not told why Titus didn't come, the record says that Paul moved forward. Was he disappointed? Yes. But Paul kept going, thankful for the assurance that the Most High "always leadeth us in triumph in Christ," according to verse 14. Not only was Paul thankful for the Lord Jesus Christ, but he was also thankful for His Mercy. A thankful spirit can triumph even though facing disappointment.

Paul also realized there were many others who needed his service. Keeping going and moving forward with God always helps and heals. When our Lord Jesus faced the tragic death of His cousin, John the Baptist, His heart was torn. But out of this wound in His own heart He fed the multitudes and healed the sick. Out of heartbreak there is healing, as we are led forward to triumph in His name.

Gladys Aylward grew up in London, England. As a

teenager she heard about the Chinese, and it changed her life. She longed to go to them and tell them of God's love. But she failed missionary training school and was told that she was not smart enough to learn the Chinese language, and they would not accept her.

Her disappointment was changed to action though, as Gladys determined that she would go to China on her own. She worked as a maid to earn travelling money. Her spirit shone brightly as she kept moving forward, carried by a dream bigger than herself. Eventually she earned enough money for her ticket to China. From then on, her drive to tell people about God's love led her to triumph over trial after trial. The small woman who failed missionary training and was told she wasn't capable of mastering a foreign language became known for all she did to help the Chinese people learn the ways of God. The story of her life was made into a movie, The Inn of Sixth Happiness, in 1958.

Where does the power come from to keep going through disappointment, defeat, and discouragement? Gladys Aylward's life showed a determination to move forward, springing from her faith in God, despite the naysayers. The lives of many others shows the amazing power of God to not only part seas and move mountains, but to strengthen you and me to do what He wants us to do.

When we hear the words "never" or "no" like Gladys Aylward did, we can remember that our God is more than able. Maybe it isn't the right time. But if it's His plan, God has no problem making a way where there seems to be no way.

Many years after I received the doctor's stinging words and received a second opinion that completely reversed the first doctor's evaluation; I faced the reality of a divorce. I knew that quickly moving into another marriage was foolish, so once more I faced the pain of blocked desires and shattered hopes of ever having my own child. But God led me, broken as I was, to explore if a single woman could adopt a baby. Upon hearing that it was possible, I slowly and almost reluctantly pursued adoption, thinking that if any baby anywhere needed a mommy, I would be overjoyed to be chosen. The adoption processes progressed quickly, and soon I was stepping on the plane to go to Russia to meet my daughter, who was then six months old.

I admit that on that long overseas flight, doubts flourished. I had already experienced the pain of broken dreams. Would this be just another heartbreak? Or would God? Could God? The familiar children's song played in my thoughts as I travelled through the night: "Jesus loves me, this I know." But how could I really know? My heart sank realizing that my faith was only a hope-so faith. I honestly hoped that it would work out for me to adopt this precious baby. Hoped.

But on that night more than twenty years ago, when

I walked out of that Russian orphanage with my little baby, I knew. It was Christmas Eve at midnight. The snow was gently falling, and it was as if the angels were singing. I knew like never before that God does know and see and care. He always knows, no matter how confusing life might be. He always cares, even when your dearest dreams lie broken at your feet. And He will give you beauty for ashes as you wait upon Him.

Learning how to keep going amidst discouragement, defeat, and depression is a discipline that I'm only beginning to learn. It takes focus. You focus on the next step. Focus on one thing you can do. Although there might be a zillion things you can't do right now, what is the one thing can you can?

In addition to focus, moving forward also takes a determination that's based on decision rather than emotion. At the point of brokenness and disappointment, it's easy to feel like you want to throw in the towel and give up. But determination responds with clear resolve. Take today to breathe and get some rest. The battle of life can be very hard and filled with unexpected changes. Breathe now. Rest and eat nutritiously today, but then tomorrow, do something. Call a friend. Take a walk. Read your Bible. Play some music. And all the while your Father works behind the scenes, to not only heal your broken heart, but to transform your mess into something good for you that brings glory to His name.

Chapter 4

Ways to Keep Going, No Matter What

Come to Me, all you who are weary and burdened, and I will give you rest. Take my yoke upon you and learn from Me, for I am gentle and humble in heart, and you will find rest for your souls. ~Matthew 11:28-29 (NIV)

It's one thing to keep going, to keep the momentum, once you've started. But it's a very different thing to keep going once you've been knocked down by life's circumstances. That was exactly how I was feeling after an adoption that I had labored to complete for years fell through. At the time I was alone in Kiev. Let me tell you how it happened.

Although my first adoption was in Russia, seven years later I was encouraged to pursue adoption in Ukraine. From the beginning it was a very different process and proceeded more slowly. But when I travel to Ukraine in 2000, I fully expected to find my little daughter. I saw a little girl that fit all my needs, so I told the facilitator that I wished to move ahead on the adoption. With joy and celebration I was taken to a nearby market where I purchased lots of cute clothing: a pink sweater and overalls, a pink jacket and hat, and the most darling pair of pink shoes. But the next morning when I was taken back to the orphanage, they said I was not able to complete the adoption.

I remember going with my facilitator to a nearby coffee shop and asking him, "Why?" All he could tell me was that sadly, it was not to be, and must look in other orphanages for an available child. It was difficult to adjust to the unexpected turn of events. I had not seen it coming, and no amount of strong coffee could ease the pain.

I went back to the flat where I was staying and walked to my room. My eyes scanned the bed where I'd placed all the new clothing to dress her in and bring her home. Tears spilled over as I sat down on the side of the bed and reached for the small pink shoes. It just didn't make any sense. Yesterday the adoption was a yes, but today it was a no. Although I was familiar with the strange roller coaster ride of international adoption, the emptiness and loss overwhelmed me. How could this have happened?

It might have been easier to accept the

disappointment of the failed adoption if I hadn't been alone, and it was hard to go from ecstasy to grief. For a long time I sat silent.

Waiting. Trying to process the sudden change of events. I began to write in my trusted journal, where I poured out my heart. I penned these words: "I will not ask why, Lord. I am beginning to learn to not question you. You have a plan for my life, and it is for my good and Your glory. I choose to trust You." And with that, I began to pack my clothes and prepare to come back to the States - with empty arms, but a full heart.

When life throws a curveball, we often struggle to regain our balance. Praying can be difficult and talking even more so. We wrestle, trying to wrap our arms around the fact that God could have prevented the pain, but He didn't. Questions fill our minds. How could a loving God allow this to happen? Does He really love me?

My mind goes to the story of Bethany Hamilton who was born in 1990. Raised in Hawaii, she longed to become a professional surfer. But a shark attack in 2003 caused her to lose her left arm and seemed initially to end her career as a rising surf champion. But one month after her accident she returned to the water and eventually won her first national title. Yes, Bethany realized her dream of becoming a professional surfing champion, but she's also been an inspiration to millions through her story of faith and determination.

So where did Bethany get the power to keep going after such a horrific experience? She admits facing fear of sharks each time she went out to surf, but she focused her thoughts on catching the waves, and she refused to dwell on the "what ifs." With determination, she worked in the water. Her adjustment to surfing with only one arm was difficult, but she persisted - day after day, one moment at a time.

In addition to accepting the accident, she has discovered some silver linings. One of those silver linings was her ability to overcome fear in scary situations and rise above difficult situations. Today she is married with a child, and a baby on the way, and continues to share her faith in Jesus Christ with a watching world. Again and again she shines the light of truth that He was the One she depended on, and she still does.

For those who struggle with questions and doubts, Bethany admits to not having all the answers. But she encourages others with the knowledge that God has all the answers, and sometimes He allows you to see some good coming from the tragedy, such as how Bethany has a huge ministry serving others in His name.

Having come to know the Lord as a young child, she leaned into Him at age 13 after the shark attack, when she faced the biggest challenge of her life. She discovered that with Him all things are possible. Energized and excited to share her courage with others, today she pours herself into helping others, particularly girls, through her charitable organization Friends of Bethany. It offers hope to overcome through Jesus Christ.

When faced with what seemed the worse, Bethany did what seemed the obvious next step: She walked back into the water, fears and all. In the process, she discovered a courage that holds up, no matter what. Yes, it was hard. Yes, she faced fears, but that's where her "one step at a time" took her, day after day. In the process she grew stronger, learned to adjust to surfing a different way, and became acquainted with the God of the impossible.

As I flew back to the States that day many years ago, I wondered what I would face. It was one thing to experience disappointment myself, but now I had a seven-year-old daughter. How could I comfort her in her grief at not having a little sister? How could I show her God's love in the midst of the unexplainable? I had no answers, but I knew God did, and that would need to be enough.

It was early evening when I arrived home and was reunited with my girl. For a long time, I just held her close. Then she looked up at me with her big brown eyes and asked the question I was waiting for: "Why?"

It's what we all long for at times. To understand. To make sense of the unexplainable. Why?

I swallowed before answering, and I stooped down to look her in the eye.

"Honey, I don't know," I said. "I just don't know. But I know that God knows, and He loves you. He knows how much you longed for a sister." By now the tears were streaming down my cheeks.

"So is that it?" she asked.

It made sense that she wanted to know if it was all over. But how could I answer that question when I had no idea? Logically it would be easy to say yes, that it was over. But there was something inside me that refused to quit. Much effort and the kindnesses of so many people had been put into this adoption. It was much too soon to say that it was done, so I pulled her closer to me.

"Well, it's done for now, but we shall just have to see what God says. He has no problem showing me the next step."

Just putting that into words gave me a sense of

peace. He did know, and until I sensed another step from Him, I would just wait. That day I put away all the toys and outfits bought for a little girl and closed the door of my heart on that dream. God would have to open it in His way and in His time if it was going to be opened at all.

Days, weeks, and months went by. While family and friends went on with their lives, it took time for my daughter and me. Sometimes we snuggled and talked about the little sister she almost had. It seemed like a bad dream. And then it came time for the talent show at my daughters' school. As we talked back and forth about what she wanted to sing, we happened upon "God Will Make A Way" by Don Moen. It was a song that I had heard years earlier, but somehow it spoke of hope and possibilities. We decided to sing it together for the school talent show.

"Do you think God will still give me a sister?" my daughter asked, after singing the words of faith again.

Yes, God could make a way where there seems to be no way. There was no doubt about that. But would I ever have the courage to step forward after the failed adoption? I didn't know. But deep in my heart I knew that God could change even that, if it was His will. I just needed to seek His guidance.

So that never-to-be-forgotten night, we stood and

sang our song of faith and trust. No matter what had happened in the past, He would make a way. He works in ways we cannot see, but He knew our hearts. He would make that dream come alive again. It was as if that song was our testimony of faith and trust. Months later on an ordinary afternoon, the phone rang. A woman from a nearby adoption agency shared that there was a little girl in need of a mother. Was I still interested? Immediately questions flooded my mind, but my answer was clear. Yes, I was very interested. That began of the process of adoption to get my second daughter from Russia. I brought my petite toddler home from Russia on February 8, 2003.

Where did the power come from? From the One who tenderly carried me through that painful and unexpected loss. From the One who gave me a season to heal and rest. From the One who birthed the love within my heart for this little girl, long before I ever saw her. Years earlier I sat alone on in the Ukraine flat grieving the sudden loss of the child I planned to adopt. Words spilled on wet pages as I wrote simple words of trust. Although I didn't understand and probably never will, I chose to trust the One who loved me. God used my simple offering of trust and gave me blessing upon blessing in the life of my precious daughter.

So as we give Him our brokenness and

disappointment and then begin doing the next obvious thing, God continues to work for our good and His glory. Behind the scenes He prepares us and works His will in ways that we can never humanly grasp, for His ways are higher than ours. But as we wait, it's important that we guard our thoughts. For all too many have missed out on His will because they didn't believe.

Chapter 5

Guard Your Thoughts

Above all else, guard your heart, for everything you do flows from it. ~Proverbs 4:23 (NIV)

Darlene Rose. Her story is one of the most amazing tales of God's protection and provision. Yes, she ranks with Corrie ten Boom as one of my favorite heroines. She was the first American woman to serve as a missionary in New Guinea along with her husband Russell. When WWII broke out, Darlene and her husband were sent to separate prison camps. Although Russell died, Darlene survived four years in prison before her release. She wrote and spoke about how her Christian faith sustained her through the worst of times.

In her autobiography, *Evidence Not Seen*, she shares an amazing story of courage, passion, and love for Jesus. Through her trials and triumphs, she experiences God's continued mercy, faithfulness, and care. In the most difficult of times the Lord kept bringing His Word to her mind, and through that she was strengthened and encouraged to realize she was never alone.

What was her secret? How did she survive such horror and loss? In her autobiography, she says she memorized Scripture from the time she was a young girl - whole chapters of God's Word. And in doing so, she was storing up His promises and truth for that time in her life when she wasn't able to read it, yet it was part of her. God's precious Word was hidden in her heart, giving her the power to keep going no matter what.

She experienced the impossible becoming possible many times, but when she was given 92 bananas while in prison, she was overwhelmed with God's goodness and provision for her. It is one thing to know that He can provide for all your needs (And my God will meet all your needs according to the riches of His glory in Christ Jesus. Phil 4:19) but another to have clear evidence of His continued power and care.

Although I've never faced anything as difficult as Darlene Rose did as a POW, I realize that in greater or lesser trials, the answer is the same: that our minds be filled with God's truth. The more we're saturated with His unchanging promises and hope, the more we experience victory in Christ Jesus. God is there. God cares. God answers prayer. God moves, especially for His faithful children.

My trials seem so small compared to suffering in a prison camp. But who of us has not experienced the pain of injustice and slander. Who hasn't dealt with the wounds of lies? At the time it seems so horrible, but God heals. Through it all, as we wisely guard our hearts to keep from becoming bitter and resentful, the Lord heals all wounds and uses it for His glory. Guarding our hearts enables us to keep moving forward in life even though the struggle is real.

Guarding our hearts involves not only recognizing the treasure of one's heart but also intentionally removing the trash from it. We must remove unforgiveness, bitterness, selfishness, and pride, so that we can run the race of life with freedom and victory. Hiding God's Word in our hearts serves as a protection when experiencing trials and difficulties, as He gives us His perspective of faith in the midst of darkness.

Nothing could have prepared me for the unexpected death of my older brother. During childhood we were very close, spending hours playing outside and climbing trees. But when he went off to college and in two years I went in another direction, we seemed to drift apart. Although infrequent, our visits were always a joy, and I can still remember the laughter of those times. I often wrote him letters to keep him up with my life and the lives of my children. I sent pictures and newspaper clippings, with a prayer that one day we would reconnect again. But one day never came.

I'll never forget that early morning phone call telling me that my brother had died most unexpectedly. For hours and days in my shock I kept thinking: never, died, final. That's it. The realization that he would no longer come to visit hit me hard. For years I had planned for that longed-for get together. From time to time I shared stories of him with my daughters to keep his memory alive. Now I grappled with the reality that future visits were not to be. Never.

At the same time my mom was declining in health and I was busy spending time with her. My brother's unexpected death made it even harder to care for my mom. Grieving over the deterioration of the health of my mom along with the sudden passing of my older brother seemed overwhelming at the time. It just didn't make sense to me. And the finality of his life seemed to knock the life out of me for awhile. But there was no time to stop. Life continued with its daily demands.

I remember in the dark of night drawing upon words of Scripture and finding its comfort. "Even though I walk through the darkest valley I will fear no evil for You are with me; Your rod and Your staff they comfort me." (Psalm 23:4) Again and again I clung to the promise of His presence and His comfort. Slowly I began to rest and adjust to what life actually was, rather than how I wanted life to be. Although it didn't bring my brother back, it gave me insight into the healing comfort that's available to everyone.

Whether it's serving time as a POW alone and far from home, or dealing with the loss of a loved one, God assures us of His help. Feelings might say that we're alone, but faith sings that His presence is an unseen reality all the time, on both the dark days and the sunny days.

There is tremendous advantage in memorizing Scripture. Like storing up food reserves for times of drought, scripture builds within one's mind a reminder of His promises. Our minds and hearts grow strong as they feed on the Truth, equipping us to withstand the toxicity of lies, doubt, and fear.

I highly recommend using a planned Scripture memory plan such as the Topical Memory System by the Navigators, or simply start with a verse or a chapter. Begin small and continue to review what you have memorized. No other practice in the Christian life is more rewarding than memorizing Scripture. Your confidence will be enhanced and your faith strengthened. Simply recalling a verse of Scripture can strengthen you to fight temptation with the beauty of Christ and His provisions.

Darlene Rose often reflected on the power that knowing Scripture gave her. Corrie Ten Boom spoke of the importance of memorizing passages in preparation for testing and tribulation. Joni Eareckson Tada encourages friends and listeners to her program to not only memorize scripture but also to apply it. Again and again, the light of truth shines on the importance of applying Scripture in order to have the power to keep going. In the process of memorizing God's Word, we are training to go the distance with strength.

Chapter 6

Training for the Distance

For the LORD God is a sun and shield; the LORD bestows favor and honor; no good thing does He withhold from those whose walk is blameless. ~Psalm 84:11 (NIV)

George Mueller lived a life that demonstrated the power to keep going again and again. He was a Christian evangelist and director of Ashley Down, an orphanage in Bristol, England, from 1805-1895. Mueller lived a life of constant dependence upon God. He relied on the Lord for all of his needs. After reading his autobiography, I was moved deeply by his faith, and how he took seriously the Lord's promise to not withhold any good thing from him. Mueller prayed about everything, and he expected each prayer to be answered.

Early on, Mueller had a reputation for being wild and disrespectful, but then he was suddenly confronted with the claims of Christ and the importance of knowing God personally. His decision to accept Jesus as his Lord and Savior radically changed his life from then on. In his journals he mentions his deep longing to study Scripture and to memorize it. Slowly God's promises became his and Mueller was transformed.

His faith was greatly tried at times, but he held tightly to his faith in God. He refused to ask men for money, but firmly believed in asking in prayer for whatever he needed. And so he did, again and again and again. He records instant after instant of God answering at the eleventh hour and always providing for all of his needs.

While Mueller read and memorized Scripture, it was his prayer life that kept him going. Mueller spent hours upon hours on his knees. During a time in England's history when orphans were left penniless and starving, Mueller took them in, clothed them, fed them, and educated them. Again and again, God poured money into his hands in answer to his believing prayer.

Like Corrie ten Boom, Darlene Rose, Joni Erickson Tada, and many others who have gone before, Mueller learned the importance of reading the Word and talking to the Lord as to a friend about all of his concerns. He was said to pray through the Scriptures as one walks through the fields. Do we wonder at the power he experienced to keep going through many trials?

He wrote of great struggles in maintaining the orphanage and providing for the needs of the children, but Mueller also shared his peace in the knowledge that God always provided. He took Matthew 6:33 to heart: to seek first the Lord and His Kingdom, and then God will supply all of your needs. For too many years I have spent worried about "What if this?" or "What if that?" but the Lord reveals in His Word that He knows exactly what we need and when we need it. As I've begun to learn to focus upon His glorious presence, gladness and trust grow within my heart. That is the secret of learning to keep going for the distance.

Years ago I sensed deep within my heart the Lord's leading to adopt a precious little girl from Russia. I was naturally concerned about my human ability to provide for her needs, but the more I prayed the greater my sense of peace that He would enable me to do all that needed to be done. But then a few years later as I prayed for the Lord to enlarge my boundaries and give me more opportunities to touch others in His name, I sensed a nudging within that there was another little girl that needed me.

I wrestled with the nudging. How could I ever raise two children as a single woman?

"Lord, this seems way too much," I said, begging for

reassurance. For days I prayed and searched His Word.

"Is anything too hard for Me?" I seemed to hear. Silly me, I thought. But pretty soon I'd begin to worry again. How could God possibly do this?

I'll never forget that trip to the beach and the early morning walks on the sand seeking the Lord's direction. I had not planned to have two children. One child was what I could manage. And I was ready to begin a doctoral program in Marriage and Family studies. I had already been accepted into the program. I had even given away all of my baby things.

"This makes no sense," I said to the Lord.

But deep within I had the strangest wrestling. More than anything I had done with my life, I loved being a mother. But how in the world could I double my responsibilities? Back and forth the struggle went. And I walked, and walked some more.

Alone beside the ocean, I poured out my fears and worries to the Lord.

And He heard my prayers.

Yes, God graciously quieted my troubled spirit and comforted me. He had never failed and He wouldn't this time. All I needed to do was to follow Him. I never heard an audible voice, and there was no writing in the sky. But a strange peace settled over my spirit and I knew the reassurance that can only come from God. Outside nothing had changed. But deep within it had been settled. I would begin an adoption again and let God lead me to the one He wanted me to mother.

As I reflect today, seventeen years later, on the way God led and provided for me, I see the importance of seeking God's will in prayer. He knows exactly what we need. He knows our deepest desire. George Mueller was moved to care for thousands of orphans in England. Although there were many times of struggle and testing, God always provided for Mueller's needs. In his journals, he wrote about times of pouring out his request to the Lord and God answering the exact need - sometimes within the hour. Surely Mueller was over his head with the huge need of all the orphans, but he never went without.

Although I only have two children to provide for, I've experienced the Lord's gracious and timely care when resources have been slim, too. Sometimes it's seemed like maybe this time we'll be abandoned, but it has never happened. No, His faithfulness and love leave me in continual praise. He has shown Himself faithful to be a Father for my two girls again and again, as I have mothered to the best of my ability.

There is so much joy in living dependent upon the Lord. His faithfulness is not only for immediate needs. No, His faithfulness is for our whole lives. He gives strength to those who are weary and power to the weak (Isaiah 40:29-31). He never leaves us. His love lasts. We only need to cultivate a life of knowing Him and seeking Him above anything else.

And our attitude is a key. When we expect God to provide and to be faithful, it seems like He delights in showering His blessings upon us.

Chapter 7

The Importance of A Positive Attitude

Finally, brothers and sisters, whatever is true, whatever is noble, whatever is right, whatever is pure, whatever is lovely, whatever is admirable - if anything is excellent or praiseworthy - think about such things.
~Philippians 4:8 (NIV)

When I think of someone who lived out the power to keep going my thoughts immediately go to Amy Carmichael. Amy was born in Millisle, County Down, Ireland in 1867. She was the oldest of seven siblings. From a young age, her unusual fascination for nature and God's creatures were evident. As a youth she gave her life to Christ, and service to Him became her center and her passion.

Amy was a risk taker and not afraid to do what she felt the Lord wanted her to do. After hearing Hudson Taylor speak, she felt called to missionary work. So she prepared first for service in China, but it was determined that her health was not good. For over a year she tried to find a place to go, but again and again it continued to be determined that her health was not good enough. No one wanted her. But filled with determination, she eventually sailed to Japan in 1893. What determination of spirit she demonstrated as she boarded that ship. The ship's captain was converted to Christianity as he observed her positive attitude in spite of the dirt and insects on board the ship.

She clung to the verse, I Thessalonians 5:16-18 "Rejoice ever more. Pray without ceasing. In everything give thanks: for this is the will of God in Christ Jesus concerning you." (KJV) Amy believed in not only reading the Word, but also applying it. The results were an obvious difference in her attitude that gave her opportunities to share her faith with others.

While in India, Amy persisted and some souls were won to Christ, but eventually she fell ill and was sent home. Amy kept going forward though. She had within her not only a call, but a power to keep going. When she was 28, she sailed to India and spent the next 56 years there without coming home. She labored to establish the Dohnavur Fellowship, an orphanage to save young girls from cult prostitution in Hindu temples. Later she took in boys as well. The Dohnavur Fellowship is still active today and includes schools and a medical clinic.

Throughout her time in India, Amy experienced many times of struggles and sadness. She not only faced the loss of friends and children, but she also lived with poor health. After a fall that broke her leg and twisted her spine, she was confined to her bed for the last 20 years of her life. During this time period she wrote most of her nearly three dozen books.

Amy's positive attitude in the face of pain and struggles continues to encourage people all over the world. Her poems and devotions reveal the insights the Lord gave her. To her, difficulties and trials were battle wounds in service of the Lord. Instead of focusing on her disappointments and losses, she continued to see them as honors in the service of her King. Poem after poem reveals her positive attitude, which has given strength, hope, and comfort to millions.

Where did Amy develop this way of seeing things? Once more I am drawn to her devotional life and the time she spent pouring over Scripture and praying. She frequently wrote about seeing each difficult experience as an opportunity, a chance to die to self. With her graceful spirit, she kept on serving the Lord, letting go of disappointments and difficulties and embracing Calvary love.

How strange it seems to hear of one who let go a focus on herself in order to follow Him fully. In contrast to our self-centered culture, Amy Carmichael's secret to her life of service was her positive, other-centered attitude developed from long hours in the Word. Prayer strengthened her to overcome and thrive in the most difficult of circumstances. Although confined to her bed for many years, she kept writing and praising the Lord. Most of her books, more than twenty of them, were written during this time period.

Amy Carmichael developed a listening ear to the Holy Spirit that strengthened her in times of trouble. When things in India grew difficult and the board advised her to return to England, Amy stayed put because she sensed the Spirit telling her to remain. Again and again she spoke of the Lord guiding her and giving her wisdom in even the most practical of things. The source of her glowing life was clearly the Lord.

Although my own life has never had the challenges that Amy Carmichael experienced, I've also faced times when relying on the Spirit has strengthened me so that I could keep going forward. My mind wanders back to years at a secular university many hours away from my family, and the one thing that kept me going was long periods of time alone with the Lord.

Left to myself, I would have been discouraged and gone home, but knowing He was with me gave me strength to endure hard, lonely times. When I experienced disappointment and discouragement, He comforted me and gave me what I needed for one more day.

My heart wanders back to when I realized my Mother's days were numbered. Once more, it was as if I had been prepared for that moment many years before. Yes, it was difficult to see her suffer and know that soon we would be parted, but deep within was a blessed assurance of His comfort and peace. Today I look forward with joy to that time when we'll be reunited in Heaven.

Times of quiet in His presence might seem strange to some people in this fast-paced society, but I've seen how the Lord uses those quiet moments to deepen our walk with Him and to teach us dependence upon Him alone. Amy Carmichael's singing faith and positive spirit are glowing examples to us today that as we keep singing and praising, He keeps strengthening us. Sometimes just a simple song or chorus will lift my heart as I go about the day. Praise lifts us to Him and turns our focus from ourselves and our needs to Him who loves us much more than we can possibly grasp.

And through intentionally fixing our thoughts on things that are true, noble, right, and lovely, the Lord works within His servants' hearts.

But we must not forget the importance of perseverance.

An attitude of perseverance empowers us to walk through fire, so to speak, and not give up. Although there are many examples of perseverance, the one that comes to my mind lived across the ocean many years before we were born.

Chapter 8

Perseverance

Let us not become weary in doing good, for at the proper time we will reap a harvest if we do not give up.
~Galatians 6:9 (NIV)

Who has never been tempted to give up? To throw in the towel? To call it quits? Although this is a human tendency, we're encouraged in the Word to keep pressing forward as we trust God. He has promised strength for each day as we depend upon Him.

William Wilberforce (1759-1833) knew how to keep pressing forward. Born to a wealthy British family he was exposed to faith at an early age by some relatives. He later turned his back on that and went on to college. There he made friends with William Pitt, who would later become Prime Minister, and was a loyal supporter of Wilberforce in his later life.

During his twenties, Wilberforce had a deep spiritual

experience and began daily Bible readings while giving up drinking and card playing. He turned his back on fashionable society. Although moved with a desire to work for social reform, he questioned whether he should continue a political life. His friend, John Newton, one of the leading Anglican churchmen of his day, encouraged him to go on with his spiritual pursuits and also continue working for social reform.

In 1789 Wilberforce addressed the House of Commons with a bill to oppose slavery. This bill was defeated, and Wilberforce spent time working to raise awareness of the evils of slavery. At this time, there was little interest in abolishing slavery. But in 1806, after the death of William Pitt, the climate changed and Wilberforce again worked to present a bill that would abolish the slave trade. As a result of hard work by Wilberforce, a bill was passed that limited about 75% of the slave trade. Then in 1807 the House of Lords and the House of Commons passed the Slave Trade Act by a huge majority. This only made the trade of slaves illegal. Wilberforce spent considerable time campaigning for the rights of slaves in Africa and other parts of the world. In addition, he worked on prison reform, education, missionary work, and public health issues.

Throughout his time fighting against slavery,

Wilberforce experienced great anguish of spirit. He hated seeing the abuse of other human beings who were made in the image of God. His efforts, which were greatly unpopular, moved to being dangerous. His position as an abolitionist caused him not only a political loss, but also ravaged his health. But Wilberforce persevered year after year. When asked why he didn't quit, he explained, "A man who fears God is not at liberty to do so." A bill abolishing the slave trade was passed three days after his death. I admire his deep Christian worldview that drove him to persistent action in the face of obvious abuses.

Where did Wilberforce get the power to keep going? It seemed to spring from his biblical worldview. Having studied Scripture, he knew God's view and worked without ceasing to break the chains that held so many people captive. Knowing God moves one to more than a life of contemplation. Rather it moves one to step out in action and to work knowing that God Himself works behind the scenes to bring about mercy, justice, and truth. The Spirit within works causing us to feel pain at the things that cause God's heart to weep and also to empower us to do what we can to bring about change.

Many years ago, after I adopted my first daughter, I began taking coursework to prepare for a career change to counseling. All around I heard the cries of people needing help - needing counseling. So while I worked full time, I also took courses at night and cared for my toddler. Looking back, the exhaustion of those days is still a faint memory, but I was moved from within by a longing to be equipped to serve Him and also a longing to have time with my daughter as she grew. I'll never forget the joy of that graduation from college, knowing that although my daughter would never remember, I'd recall the late nights and lengthy hours I spent to complete my coursework. But amidst the challenge of those hard days, memories of times of dancing in my toddler's bedroom late at night come to mind. And chocolate chip cookie parties. Laughter and playtimes together. It was as if the Lord used those longed-for times with my little girl to fill me with encouragement and energy to keep working toward the goal.

That perseverance was possible as a result of the vision I had for having more time with my daughter and a career of service for Him. It might have been easy to get distracted thinking about what I was missing in the moment, but my sights were on the goal of completion and on the Master's voice saying, "Well done!" One day at a time became my motto. Slowly the days passed, the assignments were completed, and my job was done.

During my lengthy drives to night classes, I was uplifted by worship music. And at college I met friends who encouraged and supported me in my studies while I juggled so much. Yes, it was a season of overload that eventually came to an end. But that season showed His power to enable us to do what He calls us to do. Looking back, I wouldn't have had it any other way. Through my weakness I came to know Him even better and the difficulties became opportunities for Him to show Himself faithful and true.

I'll never forget driving home from Charlottesville many years ago. It had been raining all day from Hurricane Hugo, but the university rarely cancelled classes. So with some anxiety I went to class. By the time I got out, the storm had picked up. Visibility was poor and driving had slowed to a crawl on the highway as I headed north. As I looked up ahead I noticed flashing lights and saw police cars - and the road was barricaded.

"Can't continue north, ma'am," the officer spoke through the lowered window. "Bridge is down."

I gulped.

I glanced to the right where the officer was pointing.

"Detour," he said, and moved to the next car. Rain was pouring in torrents as I drove the car in the direction I was told. It was a lonely road and immediately I wondered how long it would take me to get home to where my mom was watching my young daughter. Outside the wind howled. Inside I poured out my heart to the Lord. Alone in the storm, I managed the twists and turns of the narrow country road, but I was afraid. Nothing in my life before this had prepared me to drive in this horrible storm. Without the lights and activity of the main highway, I felt scared. But then from somewhere a verse came to mind, one that I had committed to memory many years earlier.

The Lord is my Shepherd. I shall not want.

Whispering these words quietly in the car calmed my panicky feelings and gave me courage. Never alone, I thought. I am never alone.

Minute by minute dragged by as I kept driving with my eyes glued to the narrow two-lane road. Questions taunted me. Doubts loomed. But I kept driving forward.

Though I walk through the valley of the shadow of death, I will fear no evil.

"Lord, be my comfort. Help me."

I'll never forget my joy and relief when lights shone in the distance and I realized where I finally was - about twenty minutes from home. Breathing with more ease, I maneuvered carefully. Winds tugged at my car while the rain poured, but I knew that soon I would be home.

When I parked that car that night, tears filled my eyes. My Lord had graciously answered my prayers and brought me home, and He had given me the peace of His presence each mile of the way.

Once more as I ponder the source of that power to keep going, I see the common thread. William Wilberforce carried on despite health problems and much opposition, knowing that God was with Him. Corrie ten Boom carried on day after day as a prisoner of war because her faith was in the living God. Prayer and continued meditation on memorized verses encouraged her and built her faith. Bethany Hamilton, Amy Carmichael, and many, many others have experienced a similar strengthening. The stories of His grace and deliverance are too many to number.

Chapter 9

Flexibility and Seasons

That person is like a tree planted by streams of water, which yields its fruit in season and whose leaf does not wither - whatever they do prospers. ~Psalm 1:3 (NIV)

One man who showed tremendous grace in life gives us an example of living with flexibility through all the seasons of life. He was George Beverly Shea, known as America's beloved singer of sacred song. His life was more than just about music. No, his witness has touched millions.

The name and music of George Beverly Shea was familiar to me growing up, but it wasn't until I heard him sing in person that I, too, sensed his God-given uniqueness. It was at the Billy Graham Crusade in New York City in 1960 when my attention was focused on him. He sang as he usually did right before Billy Graham gave the message, and his deep voice touched my soul. I don't remember what song he sang - The Wonder of It All or How Great Thou Art or I'd Rather Have Jesus - but it set my soul on fire with a passion to serve the Lord with all my life.

Often described as America's beloved gospel singer, Shea began singing with Billy Graham and his ministry in 1947. He may have sung before more people than any other singer. Life was filled with constant travel, both in the states and abroad. In addition, he frequently sang on "The Hour of Decision," Graham's weekly radio broadcast. Yes, he sang before millions including Presidents Dwight Eisenhower, Lyndon B. Johnson, and George H.W. Bush.

It took flexibility to go from crusade to crusade, with long nights away from home and family. As Billy Graham traveled around the globe, so did George Beverly Shea. He learned to be flexible during that season of his life. Then when his first wife, Erma Scharfe, went home to be with the Lord, he adjusted to being a widower at age 65. When he was 74, at the nudging of Ruth and Billy Graham, he met and married Karlene Aceto. Changes. Adjustments during each season of life.

But, with grace and gentleness, Shea kept moving forward, embracing the moments and singing praises to the Lord of all. What an example he left for us as we, too, face changes in our lives. Music lifts the spirits and speak truth about God's faithfulness. It has done that for me again and again. When I was growing up, my family moved frequently. When I was growing up, my family moved frequently I remember well the adjustments of new schools, new friends, and new churches. My quiet personality struggled with the constant changes, but I remember how the Lord graciously strengthened me and grew confidence within me-confidence in Him and confidence in myself. Music gave me a place where I was comfortable. Whether singing in a choir or playing the piano, I found a place where I was at home and where I belonged.

I remember those awkward years of junior high school. Day after day I walked to school and felt so alone. But then everything began to change. I discovered the junior high chorus, and then I began accompanying the chorus on the piano. That continued through all the adjustments of high school. There was always a choir to serve as pianist. I began to thrive and grow into my own the more I played the piano.

It was fitting that I played a piano solo at my high school graduation - "Rustles of Spring" by Norwegian composer Christian Sinding. Years earlier I would have been unwilling to play before so many. But at this point of my life I was beginning to stretch out of my quiet cocoon and use my ability for the enjoyment of others. Like Shea, I was learning to let go and allow the Lord to direct my paths, and when a door of opportunity opened I was willing to explore it. Letting go. Letting God.

The power that George Beverly Shea and so many others discovered, to use each season for the glory of God, became mine as I played for Him and my life slowly transformed into a life of song. His power has carried me through many changes as I've lived out his song. From singleness to marriage to being a mom, His faithfulness has caused me to rise above the burdens to live a life of overcoming. There will be more changes, if the Lord gives me life. And I know that His power will continue to be mine as I keep praying and praising

Chapter 10

Keeping Your Eyes On the Goal

I press on toward the goal to win the prize for which God has called me Heavenward in Christ Jesus.
~Philippians 3:14 (NIV)

He was born the son of Judy and Herb Chapman. Although at first Steven Chapman had his eyes set on becoming a doctor, he eventually found himself singing and writing gospel songs and eventually becoming a performer of contemporary Christian music. Chapman has become a prolific singer in his genre, having released twenty albums.

It was a cold night in November many years ago when I went to a Steven Curtis Chapman concert with some friends. It wasn't the huge crowd that amazed me that night or the quality of the music. No, it was the simple, honest sharing of his heart that touched me that night of long ago.

Chapman's music continued to touch my life as I juggled parenting my young daughter and working full time.

I remember coming home and preparing dinner in the kitchen. My daughter was by my side and suddenly we'd put on the song "Facts are Facts" and start dancing around the room. Yes, I can still hear the lyrics and the ripples of laughter. Promises are promises. Yes, facts are facts. On long drives to Charlottesville where I worked, we put in the CD and sang one after another of Chapman's songs.

Then in 2001 while I was involved with the adoption process for the second time, Chapman's song, "When Love Takes You In" was released. Sitting in my living room with my daughter, we watched the video and listened to the song with tears streaming down our cheeks. It touched the depths of my heart as I heard those words, declaring how when love takes you, in everything changes. I glanced at my eight-year-old daughter and remembered the amazing experience of bringing her home from Russia. Everything had changed, for her and for me. Now while I dealt with the unknowns of international adoption again, that truth gave me strength to keep moving forward. A miracle starts with the beating of a heart. Somewhere I knew that another little girl waited to be adopted, and that longing was powerful. I desired to have her home with me and to make my family complete, but it was to be years before that happened. I played that song and watched the video again and again.

But then in 2008 I heard the tragic news of the sudden death of Chapman's daughter, Maria. I grieved as the Chapman family shared their loss. It seemed almost unbelievable that this family who had encouraged so many in their faith should experience such great pain. Chapman himself acknowledges almost giving up singing after the death of his daughter, but in time he went on writing and singing songs of faith. The album "Beauty Will Rise" was made during this painful time of struggle. The lyrics express the questions and doubts we all know so well, along with the shining hope in Jesus Christ - Who brings beauty from ashes. Buried deep beneath our broken dreams is that hope.

Just a few months earlier I had said goodbye to my mom, and the pain of that separation ran deep. Chapman's songs of faith encouraged my heart as I saw him moving forward in faith. This is our hope. This is our promise. My heart embraced God's gift of hope and promise to me.

Later, in his book "Between Heaven and the Real World," Chapman honestly shares his heart about his steps forward, steps back, and his missteps in life. He continues to trust God for what is presently unfixable. His life shows, more than anything else, God's power to enable him to keep moving forward ... no matter what. He chose to trust God. Chapman allowed us to glimpse his vulnerabilities so we could be encouraged and strengthened. Chapman chose to do the next thing.

What a marvelous reminder that even though there are huge questions and doubts today, God will make all things new in the morning. Moving forward involves being aware of this moment and looking ahead. Moving ahead means trusting God for the unexplainable in life and embracing hope for the future. Moving ahead is looking around and doing the thing at hand: taking one simple step at a time.

Although it would be easy to simply focus on the David and Goliath victories, faith is letting God be God. We must let Him have each of our stories so He can bring beauty from all the brokenness and suffering. As we focus on the goal - Christ Jesus - our way will become possible. And there will be glimpses of beauty along the way, because He makes no mistakes.

Chapter 11

What Is Your Why?

Fixing our eyes on Jesus, the pioneer and perfecter of faith. For the joy set before Him He endured the cross, scorning its shame, and sat down at the right hand of the throne of God. ~Hebrews 12:2 (NIV)

I first came to know the name Frances Havergal when I was a child sitting at the old oak upright piano. I'd thumb through the hymnbook, back and forth, trying to find a song that was easy for me to play. And at nine that meant it had to have no sharps and no flats. One of the songs that I frequently turned to was "I Gave My Life for Thee," and my fingers played it again and again. The tune touched my heart with its simple melody. But the words. The words convicted me again and again. After all Jesus had done for me, what had I done for Him? That thought penetrated through layers of my heart, leading me into the depths of His love. I began to understand the importance of why.

As I played that song with the almost haunting lyrics "I gave, I gave my life for Thee, what hast Thou given for me" my heart responded with longing. Here was a call bigger than life. Here was a purpose beyond what I could even speak to another. All I knew was that I wanted my life to be spent serving the One who gave His life for me. How could I do less?

Born in 1836 to a Church of England minister, Frances Havergal showed great intellectual gifts, but tended to be sickly. She was a student of the Word of God and memorized whole passages of scripture. Her mother died when she was eleven, and Frances committed her life to Christ at age fourteen. Although highly intellectual and cultured, she had a simple faith and a strong confidence in the Lord. Frances had a deep prayer life, and it was said that she prayed over every line she wrote.

When she was 34, her father suddenly died. It was then that Frances wrote the consecration hymn, "Take My Life and Let it Be." In her own words, she explained that she had been on a visit staying with a houseful of others, and the Lord gave her a prayer to claim all of them for Him. She did so, and that night all of them asked Jesus into their hearts. She penned the hymn with the final line: "Ever, only, all for Thee." Frances clearly knew her "why", the purpose of her life. She was living to share her faith with others. Although not strong in body, she lived a productive and meaningful life. A glimpse of how much she accomplished in her short 42 years leaves me much to ponder.

Where did she get the power to keep moving forward, though oftentimes weak in body and sometimes bearing the sorrow in the losses of life? The why of her life had been answered early, and she lived each day for Him. Her passion was to win souls, and her energies were spent teaching Sunday School and writing letters, leaflets, and books. She discovered the importance of a full surrender to Him, and so with abandon she gave her all to Him. Her life matched the first line of her hymn:

"Take my life and let it be
Consecrated, Lord, to Thee".

Few in our day have discovered the power and the importance of that full surrender to Christ, where nothing is held back. The Lord honored Frances' desire and used her sweet spiritual radiance to touch the lives of many. Along with her consecration to Christ, she loved the Savior and was devoted to His Word. She read her Bible constantly and memorized passages, including the four Gospels. She was known for encouraging children to memorize Scripture, and she devoted regular time for prayer.

She kept a habit of praying three times a day. And with a paper in her Bible on which she wrote the subject of her prayers, she carefully recorded initials of loved ones and friends. Hers was not the rush-in-and-out kind of prayer life. Instead she seriously pursued and inspired many others to pray with deep devotion. Clearly this was a source of great power for her that enabled her to keep going throughout all the ups and downs of life.

I can still hear the simple chords of "I Gave My Life for Thee," written by Frances Havergal many years ago and played by my youthful fingers. The words of commitment speak truth to me today and inspire me and others to press deeper into knowing Him. She discovered how to press forward through sad times and busy times, through days of grief and moments of joy. Frances leaves us a clear example of the importance of listening to the heart of the Father. His call for today remains and also His power to overcome whatever comes our way.

Chapter 12

Others Who Discovered the Power to Keep Going

For you created my inmost being; you knit me together in my mother's womb. ~Psalm 139:13(NIV)

Whether examining the lives of people from the past or present, we continue to see a marvelous thread of strength in spite of tremendous struggles and hardships. But what do you do when suddenly your world turns completely upside down? Join me as we look at the life of another who knows what it is to be carried by the Lord through the worst of times. One woman who pressed through pain into healing is Christine Caine. Not only did she have to work through the scars of abuse, but when she was 33 she learned she was adopted as an infant. In one moment, she discovered everything she had believed about her life was untrue. Her brother was adopted at a young age as well. While trying to process this news, she was drawn to Psalm 139 where she was reminded that even though she didn't know the specifics about her birth, God knew. The marvelous truth of His knowing gave her comfort and security during a challenging time.

God's intentions were to bring good from what she experienced and to use it for His glory. In 2008 she and her husband founded the A21 Campaign that fights human trafficking. Today she is sought after as an international speaker and a faith giant. She could have stayed hidden and turned away from God's call to serve Him. It might have been easier for her to have chosen a less public role, but she continues to live out her faith with boldness today. Instead of accepting her scars as something to be ashamed of, she sought healing and discovered that the Lord is faithful and true. She allows God to use all the broken pieces of her life, and it's a joy to see what He is doing in and through her. No problem, no issue is too big for Him to use for His glory and our good. As she leans upon the One who knows all about her, she continues to experience His healing grace in her life.

How true it is that nothing is hidden from our God. He knows our deepest thoughts and secrets. He knows what we don't even understand about ourselves, but as we give Him all of our brokenness He creates healing and new life. And He gives us the strength to keep moving forward in His power.

My mind wanders to Hudson Taylor, who was born in 1853. As a teenager he accepted the Lord as his personal Savior and felt God's call to take the gospel to China. After a season of preparation, he arrived in China with a desire to build relationships with the people. He made a radical decision. He adopted their clothing and wore a pigtail, much to the consternation of the missionaries already there. But Taylor pressed on, intent on taking the Gospel to the interior of China.

When the mission organization could no longer pay him, Taylor resigned and continued on trusting the Lord to meet all of his needs. He labored intensely to the point of needing to return to England for a season, and he admitted to having doubts. But the Lord met him right where he was. He surrendered himself afresh to the Lord, giving Him all of his doubts and worries. From then on, Taylor moved forward, and within a year he left once more for China.

His boldness knew no bounds. His work ethic and absolute trust in God inspired scores to leave the comforts of the West to take the Gospel to the vast and unknown region of the interior China. Through death, sickness, extreme hardships, loss of children, and being misunderstood and criticized, Taylor moved forward in God's strength.

I was most interested in a letter that Hudson Taylor wrote to his sister, Amelia. He told her he had discovered the importance of receiving God's fullness in exchange for his weakness. He explained that faith was the substance of things hoped for and the reality upon which you can rest. He shared the importance of grasping oneness in Christ and the difference that that truth made to him. As if for the first time, he grasped the concept of resting in Christ - not striving. He knew the important thing wasn't his own efforts, but resting in what Christ had done and was doing through him.

Suddenly the work that had been overwhelming and crushing became lighter. He discovered the wonder of the exchanged life: Christ for his life. What a secret that still is today.

Years ago I became familiar with E. Stanley Jones. I found a worn copy of *Abundant Living.* It's collection of readings that encouraged and inspired readers to experience more in their lives. I found his writings stirred my longing for more, so I explored used bookstores looking for his books. Today I have about six of his books and frequently reread them. In one of his books, he shares his experience as a new missionary to India, and the importance of surrendering to the Lord Jesus.

E. Stanley Jones discovered the transforming power of Christ and the importance of living a life of continually surrendered to Him. Like those who lived before him, he faced challenges and battles throughout his life, but he lived his life abiding in Christ. Even after he experienced a stroke later in his life, he continued to preach the Gospel.

If you're interested in learning more about the power that Jones discovered - the power to keep going - he describes an experience he had in Lucknow, India. It was a crisis experience, and he was exhausted and feeling overwhelmed by the needs all around. He felt a voice saying to him, "If you turn over to Me what you are worrying about, I will take care of it." Jones took the bargain and released all the stress and worry he had been carrying. From then on, he kept a rigorous teaching and writing schedule without missing a step. He surrendered the burdens and found peace.

Another who discovered power to keep going was Fanny Crosby, an American poet and hymn writer. Crosby, sometimes known as the Queen of Gospel Songs, was born to John and Mary Crosby in 1820. When she was six weeks old she came down with a cold and inflammation in her eyes. Although there had been thoughts that maybe a doctor's prescribed treatment caused her blindness, others seem to think it was congenital just hadn't yet been noticed. Before she was born, the Lord planned her life of service.

As a young girl she memorized huge passages of scripture. At fifteen, she enrolled in the New York Institute for the Blind and learned to play the piano, organ, harp, and guitar. She also developed her beautiful voice. Fanny became involved advocating for the blind and teaching. While in the beginning she wrote secular songs, after her conversion she began writing only sacred hymns. With an amazing speed she wrote song after song, working with various song writers including, William Bradbury, Philip Bliss, Robert Lowry, and Ira Sankey. Her hymns were filled with hope, and story after story is told of how God used those songs.

Fanny is well-known for writing "Safe in the Arms of Jesus," "Blessed Assurance," and "Saved by Grace." In addition to writing under her own name, she also wrote prolifically under pseudonyms. Fanny never allowed her handicap to keep her from a life of full service to the Lord encouraging and inspiring others. Although she married, her only child died in infancy. Fanny continued writing gospel hymns, speaking, and doing home mission work. Even in her elderly years, she encouraged others, always drawing upon her faith.

She didn't see her blindness as a handicap, but something the Lord allowed in her life to enable her to see Him. From the time she was a young girl; Fanny embraced her blindness and refused to become negative or to see herself as a victim. She accepted it as God's will for her life, and consistently radiated peace and joy. Her understanding of God's personal love for her went deep and that influenced how she viewed her life. Nothing was an accident. With determination she worked hard to be independent and useful. As a result, our world was gifted with an abundance of gospel hymns that still bless many even today.

Today, all too often, people view handicaps as weaknesses that are limiting. Fanny shared again and again that if she had a choice, she'd still prefer to have lived blind so that her Jesus would be the first face she would look upon. There is no doubt that her healthy mindset contributed greatly to the fruitful life she lived. Contentment was her crown.

That reminds me of another well known woman in our time, Elisabeth Elliott. She married Jim Elliott at a young age, and the couple went to Ecuador as missionaries to the Quichua Indians. Her husband along with four other missionaries was killed by members of another remote tribe called the Aucas. Elisabeth was left with a 10-month-old little girl and eventually lived for two years with the Aucas. Instead of allowing herself to become overwhelmed with grief and disappointment, she viewed her husband's death as having been allowed by her loving Father.

Elisabeth Elliott's perspective influenced her ability to keep moving forward. What was the source of her perspective? Her mind and soul were saturated with God's truth, and she drew upon that in her most vulnerable moments. Most people would have jumped the first ship to get home to safety and comfort. Most moms would have wanted to protect their daughter from any possible harm, particularly after the loss of a husband.

But Elisabeth Elliott was not like most people. Nor was Corrie ten Boom or Fanny Crosby. Like the others who pressed toward the call of Christ in their lives, they experienced the amazing strength and protection that only He can give. And He promises that to all who trust in Him.

Some of those we've mentioned grew up in Christian homes and were exposed to the truth of His Word from early on. Others only came to know Him later in life.

The ability to keep moving forward through the harshest of situations is not about economic background. Some of those poorest by human standards are the strongest in standing firm on His promises. Yes, some of those who seem to have the least are the richest in faith.

One day I received a letter from someone that would eventually become a dear friend. Emily Ann read an article of mine that was published, and then she wrote to me. I was touched by her kindness in writing and noticed that she lived in the college town where I had spent many years. Thus our friendship began, and back and forth our letters went. Over time, I learned something of her world and what was most important to her. Although living very simply, she always had a positive, encouraging attitude that radiated joy and satisfaction. Her letters were often accompanied by a simple bookmark or newspaper clipping. And she took interest in my busy life as a single parent.

Emily Ann became one of my trusted prayer warriors. Whenever I had a need, I asked her to join me in prayer, and I knew that she took my concern to the Father. We shared joys and sorrows. Emily Ann lived out love and friendship, and I am the richer for that. She also lived out a life that knew the power to keep going. When she wasn't able to leave her small apartment anymore due to sickness, she continued to accept even that with grace, always focusing on His blessings to her.

I'll never forget the call a few weeks before she

passed, where she shared her heart and peace in knowing that her Father was with her through everything, and that with Him she would triumph. We spoke about seeing each other one day and that precious hope we both had that there would be a day when we would see Jesus face to face. My heart ached but my spirit rejoiced, knowing that my dear friend was not only at peace, but also continuing to anticipate the Glory that was before her.

Emily Ann was like so many quiet people of faith who simply live it out wherever they are. Newspapers never write their stories, and they seem to silently pass without much notice. But when you linger awhile and ponder the steady life of love and faithfulness, you sense that for a time you were in the company of royalty. That's how it seemed with Emily Ann. A humble servant who avoided the attention or praise of others, she lived knowing the One who died for her and lived in her heart. And knowing that gave her strength and staying power that withstood the trials and difficulties of life.

Chapter 13

Your Story and Mine

No, in all these things we are more than conquerors through Him who loved us. ~Romans 8:37(NIV)

I've never thought of myself as a conqueror or a warrior. A few months ago in a group discussion someone referred to me as being a fierce warrior. It surprised me then and still does. Although I can be quite passionate about the ones dearest to me, I don't see myself as a warrior.

But upon glancing back at my own story, I'm beginning to glimpse that part of me that acts like a conqueror, rising above the challenge to overcome. Yes, looking back helps, because in the moment I rarely see anything remotely close to this. Maybe my mind and heart are so focused on simply living a life of integrity and purpose that it eludes me. So join with me as I look back. Then I welcome you to look back in your own life and see if you can detect the smallest indication of that power to keep going in the hardest of times.

Life seemed to develop a steady rhythm as I grew into my adult years. I enjoyed not only my teaching career and my work with children, but also serving the Lord within the church as Sunday school teacher, organist, and pianist. Although I longed to be married and to have my own little cape cod house surrounded by a white picket fence and filled with children, my life was busy with service, and I was content. I remember that day that I knelt by my bed praying for greater faith. I hungered to grow in boldness. I wanted the Lord to use me in any way He chose, but I had no idea what was ahead. All that I knew was that my heart said "Yes!" to Him. With that decision there was peace.

Just a few months later I met the man I would later marry.

Soon after we were married my life took a downward spiral, and all my hopes and dreams crumbled to pieces. I found myself divorced and completely broken.

Again and again, I cried out to the Lord, "Why?" It didn't make sense, but there was no denying the writing on those papers. Divorce.

For days I struggled to go on. Sleep gave me some rest from the constant thinking and questioning. But as soon as I'd awaken in the early morning hours I would remember.

"Where are You, Lord?"

On an intellectual level I understood, but on a spiritual level the struggle raged as I fought a battle simply to go on with life. The heart shattered does not so quickly recover. And while on the outside I began to pick up some pieces of normalcy, a numbness - the result of deep pain - was evident within. My relationship with the Lord that previously had been real and precious now felt flat and lifeless.

Power to go on? No, there was no power, at least not that I was aware of. I simply existed, with many questions, doubts, and wounds. But the disciplines that I had developed early in life stayed with me. Although for a while I wasn't able to concentrate for long periods of time, I sat with my open Bible. A word here or a word there caught my attention and poured what was like oil on my aching wounds. Verses that I had hidden in my heart as a young child in Sunday School came to mind and ministered comfort and peace.

Slowly life became a little less difficult, but the question was still there.

"Why, Lord? I just don't understand."

It was truly a crisis of faith for me. Many hours were spent kneeling in prayer where only sobs could be heard.

Alone, I wept, and there seemed to be no answer.

I took a part-time job and began working with preschool children. Hearing their laughter and being with them day after day restored my sense of a routine.

But those painful questions came at the most unexpected times.

"Where were you, Lord? You heard my prayers. Why, Lord?"

Looking for something to fill my time and to ease those constant unanswered questions, I joined a Precept Bible Study Class on Habakkuk. I can still remember the first time I read these words:

Though the fig tree does not bud
and there are no grapes on the vines,
though the olive crop fails
and the fields produce no food,
though there are no sheep in the pen
and no cattle in the stalls,
yet I will rejoice in the LORD,
I will be joyful in God my Savior.
~Habakkuk 3:17-19

My heart beat in response. Here was something that I could do. Although within I felt that I had nothing left, and that my hopes and dreams were dashed, I could intentionally give praise to the Lord. Yes, I not only could do that, but I would.

So from that moment on, I began to make a point of praising the One who had always been so close and real to me. I wrote out my thoughts of praise and began to pray with a slowly beating heart that longed for Him again.

One afternoon as I drove home from work, a song began to play and I reached to turn up the dial. It spoke of a time when you feel you're going under and there is no hope. Tears welled up in my eyes. It was as if the song was especially for me: my song of heartbreak. Once more the chorus swelled into a theme of praising the Lord. And I listened to the reminder that those very things that seemed to threaten your very life - those chains - would become powerless as you praised the Lord.

I hadn't been looking for that word, but it was sent to encourage me and to direct me in what to do. Behind the scenes, God continued to work to heal me and to show me what to do. So I continued to praise Him for who He was, even though I didn't understand. Day after day, I lifted my broken heart to Him. Night after night, I went to bed knowing that He was with me.

Then one day I was talking with a friend who knew my longing for a child of my own.

"You can always adopt," she encouraged. At that moment I didn't have the heart to look into anything.

But she placed a phone number in my hand, and I slipped it into my pocket. It was days later that I happened to find that little piece of paper and decided to go ahead and make that call. The woman with whom I spoke quickly assured me that singles not only could adopt, but that those adoptions were moving quickly. She offered to send me some paperwork that I could look over.

Over the next few weeks I poured over home study papers with the thought of possibly adopting. Where did the power come from to begin to wade through all the forms and go through all the visits? Only God could have given it to me.

Many an evening I sat on the floor of the living room spinning the globe around. The adoption agency wanted to know where I wanted to go to adopt a child. But for me it was always a question of where the Lord would possibly have a child that He would want me to parent. I was willing to go anywhere. Just the thought of holding my own little sweet-smelling baby girl stirred within me that dream that had been broken into a million pieces. It was now being resurrected.

Days moved quickly between work and preparations

for a possible international adoption. Although at first I prepared to go to Guatemala, I was suddenly told to do the paperwork again in preparation to go to Russia. In a way, the thought of traveling abroad to adopt a little baby girl seemed unreal. But when a picture of the most beautiful little baby girl with big eyes was put in my hand, the dream began to take on the form of reality. Suddenly it hit me: This could really happen.

"But, Lord, will this dream be crushed too?" I wondered.

Doubts arose. I was fearful of going through another heartbreak. But if I didn't try, I would never know. I wrestled deep within and determined to keep praising the Lord. After all, before Him the chains that hold us captive drop powerless. One more day. Another step forward. Waiting. Wondering.

Finally the day came when I boarded the plane to travel to Russia to get my baby girl and to complete the adoption. My faith shook as I faced my deepest fears and walked forward. What if she wasn't even available? My trust had been shattered before. Was I going to experience another disappointment?

How could I trust the One who allowed me to go through such deep sadness? All that I knew was that in the midst of all my suffering, He was there. He knew all about it and He Cared. Although I might never understand, I knew that He did. Somehow I knew His presence was enough. No matter how things worked out, I had to try.

From the first moments when I landed in Moscow, I saw God's provision for me. There was a strange calm that surrounded me. And I didn't feel alone. That in itself was most unusual.

"Is she available? Is she here?" I kept asking, wanting to be reassured that the child I was longing to adopt, the one whose black-and-white picture was in my purse, was still waiting for me.

"Da. Da." I kept being told "yes," in Russian, and I relaxed a little. Before I knew it I was guided to the train for the overnight trip to the region where my child's orphanage was located. I always thought of her as my little girl. Call it fear or faith, I could not imagine not getting her.

Early the next day I stepped off the train, sleepy but excited. This would be the day I saw my baby for the first time. Deep inside, I often whispered prayers. Strangely the familiar children's chorus ran through my mind: Jesus loves me. Yes, I thought. I know He loves me but I don't know ... and there I seemed to stop. It was impossible for me to put my doubts and fears into words.

At the orphanage I was led into a small nursery. It was so tiny that I could hardly turn around. As I stood there feeling awkward and alone, a Russian nurse came and placed in my arms a tiny baby girl. I looked down at her, and my heart somersaulted with pure joy. The same dark eyes that I had looked at for months. Oh what a beauty she was. She looked at me with all seriousness and reached for my nose as if to say, "You're mine."

Suddenly I began to hum that familiar chorus - the one that had been singing in my head for days - Jesus Loves Me. Drawing her close, I softly sang over her. Yes, Jesus loves me. Yes, my heart beat strongly. He did love me. He did. Tears filled my eyes as I whispered those words again. Yes, Jesus loves me.

This child that I held in my arms was placed there by the One who always loved me. She was given to me by the very One with whom I struggled to trust. None of it made sense. But then again, it all began to make sense. Clearly He showed me His presence and power. I would never have been able to mother this little one if I had not walked through that painful season, and I simply couldn't imagine my life without her.

The clock seemed to stop that afternoon of our first

meeting so long ago. The details are etched in my memory, although many years have passed. Her fixed stare. My tears of joy. Singing over her. Knowing … yes, knowing that He loves me. No matter how different it might look at times. The threads of pain and suffering are woven with the threads of joy and grace. Together He weaves beauty from the ashes of heartbreak, disaster, and loss. He breaks through the thick walls of misery and sickening agony and shines the light of His presence in a way that we can't possibly miss it.

A few days later, I walked out of that orphanage holding a little baby wrapped in a soft pink blanket. Christmas Eve. As I looked up, the snow was gently falling, and it was as if I heard the angels singing. He loves you. He always has. He always will.

Doubt and brokenness are part of our life here on earth, but He is stronger than anything that comes against us. His Word continually speaks of resurrection, reconciliation, and the afterward of joy. And that doesn't just refer to heaven someday, but also in the now. In His time He sings over our scars and brokenness with His song of love. "Arise," He says. "This is your time."

I'm grateful that He graciously allowed me to glimpse the healing of His love. Had I never experienced the previous suffering, I would never have known my present joy. His love for each one of us is much deeper and more intimate than we can possibly understand. He sees. He knows. He understands. And we can trust Him to be faithful and true, no matter what we face in this life. Nothing can separate us from His Love. That truth stands strong. The truth of His unchanging love anchors us through the changes we face in life.

Those days and weeks and months of crying out to Him, "Why?" without an answer were worth it all. Because while it seemed like nothing was happening, He was working behind the scenes in love, preparing His gift for me. During those difficult times when I didn't see how I could ever go forward in life, He was planning for me and being the greatest gift of all to me.

There have been other challenging, painful times in my life, just as I'm sure there have been in yours. This was just one of the hardest for me. Through this experience, I began to see where the power to keep going comes from. It doesn't come from self-help books or from keeping busy. It didn't come through avoiding or denying the pain. No, the power came through being so weak in my own strength that I was forced to lean on Him with everything that I had. I desperately needed Him. He graciously held me when I couldn't even utter a prayer or read a passage of the Word. He tenderly watched over me, just giving me one thing at a time to do.

Answers did not pour in with abundance. As a matter of fact, for months I had no indication of His presence. Pain blocked me from sensing anything of faith. And those doubts bombarded my mind with questions that simply had no response.

But there came a time when I imagined it was Him wrapped in a blanket looking up at me. Tears washed away all the doubts and sorrow. I could not go back, and I still had to accept what was. But He gave me something to do for Him - a high and holy calling. Just mother this little girl for Him.

My story is different from yours. But if you're like many folks you, too, have experienced heartbreak and disappointment. You, too, have known what it is to lose something dear and precious to you. And maybe you've had a time when you struggled to just go on.

Take a few moments and reflect on your unique story, even if it's been years since you've experienced it. As we ponder that time together, let's see if you've had any of the same struggles that others in this book have known. Grab a cup of coffee or tea and as you think back, just jot down some of your thoughts here.

What was the hardest part about your struggle?

Where did you turn in the moments of your despair?

How was your faith impacted?

At our greatest point of need, God is always there. But sometimes we aren't looking for Him, and many times the pain we're experiencing blocks us from sensing His presence. How did your faith help you through your pain?

Frequently in the midst of heartbreak, we're not even able to verbalize a prayer. But whether we can or not, He knows our need. What is your heart's prayer?

Many times people are helped by reading Scripture or a listening to a song. A particular song about praising the Lord touched me driving home one afternoon, and it penetrated the wall around my broken heart. What touched you during your difficult journey?

I found that only upon looking back could I begin to see His marvelous protection and love for me. If you are some distance from that difficult time in your life, what can you see now, as you look back?

Maybe you're struggling at this moment with a heartbreak, devastating loss, and pain. Maybe every day is an uphill battle for you. The One who loves you with an everlasting love wants you to lean upon Him. Talk with a trusted friend or counselor.

Conclusion

I have told you these things, so that in me you may have peace. In this world you will have trouble. But take heart! I have overcome the world. ~John 16:33 (NIV)

Although we wish it wasn't so, trouble seems to come to all. Life has its unpredictable twists and turns that leave us struggling for balance and looking desperately for a way to get through. Many times these difficulties couldn't have been avoided even if we'd had advanced warning. But there is a way to overcome trials. Like some of the people mentioned in this book who looked to a Savior and Lord to help them, we can discover that indescribable and unexplainable power that sustains us through the worst times we can imagine.

It's a power that comes from a personal relationship with the living Lord. It is a power that doesn't run in defeat or give in to fear. No, the power that is in the Lord is strong and works for us in ways that we might not even realize.

We're surrounded on all sides, it seems, by people who are facing their hardest challenges. We have often heard the phrase, "It's not what happens to you; it's what you do with it." There's a difference in the person who is overcome by troubles and trials and the one who gradually begins to rise up with faith and keeps going forward. Although some personalities face unexpected struggles with a more positive attitude, the one who turns to faith in the all-seeing, all-knowing, all-loving God grows stronger a little at a time. For it is in our helplessness that we're able to receive His power. It's when we're at the end of our own plans and projects that He begins to work.

In our culture, we champion independence and self-sufficiency, but in truth it is in the getting to the end of ourselves that opens us up to receive power and presence. Like the poor leper in the Bible who called out to Jesus, it's in reaching out to Him that we discover He's been reaching out to us all along.

Again and again, I hear stories of people coming to the end of themselves with broken health, financial problems, relationship struggles, work pressures, grief, and loss. They tried and tried on their own to fix themselves but to no avail.

Nothing worked. Yes, they faced the unbelievable consequences, but still could not fix their problems. Pressure upon pressure mounted.

Sadly, some of these folks give up for lack of a better alternative. But others discover the amazing, life-changing power that is available to all. It begins with discovering a personal relationship with the Lord of all. It's in knowing Him and admitting our own weakness to fix ourselves that we begin to discover His amazing transforming power. It is in taking the following steps that we can begin to knows and experience a power beyond all earthly power.

1. **Admit your need for a Savior and Lord.**
   Romans 3:23 says that all have sinned and come short of the glory of God. Accepting and admitting your own sinfulness and need of a Savior opens the way for Him to enter your life and transform what was once a journey without life, hope, and eternal purpose.

2. **Believe that Jesus is the One and only Savior and Lord.**
   Acts 16:31 says to, "Believe in the Lord Jesus Christ

and you will be saved". It's an amazing promise of hope for all. Receive the gift of His sacrifice - His shed blood - for your sins. In order to know The power of His life within you, you must know the power of His Blood, for it brings pardon, justification, and boldness when you approach God. Yes, you cannot know the power of the Spirit until you know the power of the blood.

3. **Confess your sins and accept Him**.

Discover all the power of the Holy Spirit as you study His Word. The secret of effective Christian living is knowing the power of the Spirit through the Word of God. the Spirit reveals Christ, the Spirit convicts, and The Spirit renews. When you accept Jesus into your heart, the Holy Spirit takes up residence in your life. Realizing that you are indwelt by the Spirit of God - that He lives within you - is a glorious thought. And this same Spirit satisfies and gives freedom. He is a fountain springing up within you, pouring the indescribable joy of His living water into your soul.

4. **It's your privilege to experience victory in life.** The Holy Spirit strengthens you with power as you surrender your life to Him. Ephesians 3:16-19 (NIV) refers to the amazing strengthening and victory that the believer is promised:

   I pray that out of His glorious riches He may strengthen you with power through His Spirit in your inner being, so that Christ may dwell in your hearts through faith. And I pray that you, being rooted and established in love, may have power, together with all the Lord's holy people, to grasp how wide and long and high and deep is the love of Christ, and to know this love that surpasses knowledge - that you may be filled to the measure of all the fullness of God.

   This strengthening comes after surrendering all. Looking back over the lives of Christians that received power going through the hardest of times, and you can see a time in their lives when they did exactly that. Eric Liddell spoke the truth as he explained where the power came from to run so fast. God honors those who honor Him. As you place Him first in your life, you'll begin to discover the truth of His Word.

5. **Emptying must come before filling.**

   You must empty yourself of your own will and your own plans, so you can be filled with His will and with His plans for your life. He will teach you daily what His will is when you read the Bible. Just like with food, yesterday's filling cannot satisfy today's needs, so you must daily be taught by the Spirit of God what His Will is. Spend time alone with the Lord, praying and feeding on His Word. Yes, God uses people and groups to build up His church, but you must abide with Him alone and hold fast to that discipline. He's willing to make His will clear to you and longs for you to draw close to Him constantly.

6. **Live life in complete dependence upon the Holy Spirit.**

   God doesn't want you to live depending solely upon your natural temperaments. No, He wants to empower you with power from Him and lead you to do so much more than you can possibly imagine. He will do everything for you as you let Him do it.
   Yes, power belongs to God and it's available for

everyone that asks. Power belongs to God (Psalm 62:11) and you can have it for the asking. God says, just hold out your hands and I will give it to you (Matthew 7:7, 11).

The power that Eric Liddell and many others discovered is real and available to all. It comes from seeking The Lord in prayer and trusting Him to answer. There is no magic wand, and many have waited for years for His answer. But God is faithful. He will not turn away from you. Instead He will bend toward you in your need and lift your load as you place it in His hands. His amazing power will lift you above negative circumstances and give you wisdom in how to face each new day. His presence will cheer you on with the wonder that you are never alone. The more we seek Him the more we will discover His presence.

Yes, your prayers today can accomplish just as much as prayers of people from the past. You can meet every temptation victoriously through prayer. You can face any heartbreak and devastation victoriously through prayer. You can rise and experience the wonder of His healing power as you pray, trusting Him to do for you what you cannot do yourself. No matter what the situation, you can be a man or woman of power as you pray.

Power belongs to God (Psalm 62:11), so if you're

longing for power to keep going in life, turn to the Lord wherever you are and seek from Him what only He can give.

The more I examine the lives of people who have overcome, the more I see the thread of faith and its importance. Wherever you are, no matter what has happened in your past, turn to the Lord Jesus Christ. He will never turn you away. His love is everlasting, and He is waiting for you. Then you, too, will know the joy of His presence and power for every day.

Resources

Aylward, Gladys, as told to Christine Hunter. *Gladys Aylward: The Little Woman.* Chicago:
Moody Press, 1970.

Boom, Corrie ten. *Don't Wrestle, Just Nestle.* Old Tappan, New Jersey: Revell, 1971.

Davis, Rebecca. *Fanny Crosby: Queen of Gospel Songs.* Published by Journey Forth, 2003.

Elliot, Elisabeth. *A Chance to Die*. Old Tappan, New Jersey: Revell, 1987.

Elliot, Elisabeth. *Through Gates of Splendor*. Carol Stream, Illinois: Tyndale Momentum, 1956.

Havergal, Frances. Kept for the Master's Use. Baker Book House: Originally published 1879.

Jones, E. Stanley. *A Song of Ascents*. Nashville: Abingdon Press, 1979.

Lawson, J. Gilchrist. *Deeper Experiences of Famous Christians*. Anderson, Indiana: Warner
Press, 1981.

Liddell, Eric. *The Disciplines of the Christian Life.* Nashville: Abingdon Press, 1985.

Pierson, A.T. *George Muller of Bristol.* Grand Rapids, MI: Kregel, 1999.

Piper, John. *Amazing Grace in the Life of William Wilberforce.* Wheaton, Illinois: Crossway Books, 2006.

Rose, Darlene. *Evidence Not Seen.* HarperOne, 2003.

Shea, George Beverly. *How Sweet the Sound.* Carol Stream, Illinois: Tyndale House, 2004.

Steer, Roger and Billy Graham. *J. Hudson Taylor.* UK: OMF, 2001.

Steer, Roger. *George Muller: Delighted in God.* UK. Christian Focus Publications, 2006.

Tada, Joni Eareckson. *Joni: An Unforgettable Story.* Grand Rapids, MI: Zondervan, 2001.

Wilberforce, William. *A Practical View of Christianity.* Peabody, Mass: Hendrickson Publishers, 1996.